Elijah
asks for bread

Story by Penny Frank
Illustrated by Tony Morris

THE LION
STORY BIBLE

21

TRING · BELLEVILLE · SYDNEY

The Bible tells us how God chose the Israelites to be his special people. He made them a promise that he would always love and care for them. But they must obey him.

Elijah was a prophet, someone who told the Israelites what God wanted them to hear. But sometimes the Israelites did not listen. They wanted to disobey.

You can find this story about Elijah in your own Bible in the first book of Kings, chapter 17.

Copyright © 1984 Lion Publishing

Published by
Lion Publishing plc
Icknield Way, Tring, Herts, England
ISBN 0 85648 746 5
Lion Publishing Corporation
10885 Textile Road, Belleville,
Michigan 48111, USA
ISBN 0 85648 746 5
Albatross Books
PO Box 320, Sutherland, NSW 2232, Australia
ISBN 0 86760 530 8

First edition 1984

Reprinted 1984, 1985

Printed and bound in Hong Kong
by Mandarin Offset International (HK) Ltd.

**British Library Cataloguing in
Publication Data**

Frank, Penny
Elijah asks for bread. – (The Lion
Story Bible; 21)
1. Elijah – Juvenile literature
I. Title   II. Morris, Tony
222'.530924   BS580.E4

ISBN 0-85648-746-5

**Library of Congress Cataloging in
Publication Data**
1. Elijah, the prophet—Juvenile
literature. 2. Prophets—Palestine—
Biography—Juvenile literature.
3. Bible. O.T.—Biography—Juvenile
literature. [1. Elijah, the prophet.
2. Bible stories—O.T.] I. Morris, Tony,
ill. II. Title. III. Series: Frank, Penny.
Lion Story Bible; 21.
BS580.E4F67 1984   222'.5309505
84-17092
ISBN 0-85648-746-5

The Israelites were having trouble with their king. He should have been telling them to obey and love God.

Instead he served a god called Baal. He even punished the Israelites if they obeyed their own God.

The king's name was Ahab.

So God sent the Israelites a prophet called Elijah. God often spoke to the prophet, and then Elijah told the Israelites what God had said.

One day God gave Elijah a message for
King Ahab.

'God says he will stop sending the
rain, because you are so wicked. He
will send it again when you learn to
obey him.'

The king was very angry.

The rivers and wells dried up because there was no rain.

The king was very thirsty. So were all the people.

The king was so angry that Elijah ran
away to the town of Zarephath.
God told Elijah that he had just the
right people for him to stay with in
Zarephath.

God told Elijah that he would stay with
a tiny poor family, just a mother with
a little boy.

God said, 'You will be safe there.'

Elijah did not know where to find the family but as he came into the town of Zarephath he saw a woman.

She was picking up sticks to make a fire. She looked tired and sad, and very poor.

Elijah spoke to her.

'I am so hungry and tired,' he said. 'I would love a drink of water and a small piece of bread. Do you think you could go and get them for me?'

The woman looked very surprised.

'Don't you know there has been no rain?' she said. 'Nothing will grow. There has been no harvest here for a long time.'

The woman told Elijah, 'All I have is
a handful of flour and a spoonful of oil.
I shall make a meal with it on this fire
for myself and my little boy. Then it
will all be gone and we shall starve.'

Elijah said, 'If you will use the flour and the oil to make a meal for me you will see that God will care for you.'

The woman took Elijah to her home.
She took the flour and the oil out of
her cupboard. She mixed them together
and patted them between her hands
into little cakes. Then she cooked them.

The woman took the little meal to Elijah. She almost cried as she watched him eat it.

'What will I give to my little boy now?' she asked.

But when she looked in the bowl she had a big surprise. There was still the same amount of flour left.

Then she looked in the jar. There was still a spoonful of oil.

So every day the mother made a meal
for Elijah, her son and herself.

Every day when they had finished
the meal she looked in the bowl. There
was the same amount of flour left.

Then she peeped into the jar. There
was always the same amount of oil.

One day the little boy was very ill. He was so ill that he died. The mother was so sad.

'There is no one for me to love now,' she said to Elijah. 'I have taken care of you, so why has God let this happen?'

Elijah lifted the boy off his bed.
'Let me take him away for a little
while,' he said.

He took the boy up to his own room.
He put him down on his bed. Then he
shut the door. He wanted to talk to God.

'Why have you let this happen?' he asked God. 'Please make the boy better because his mother has been so kind.'

God heard Elijah talking to him. He made the boy alive again. Elijah could see him breathing.

Elijah took the boy downstairs.

'Look,' he said to the mother. 'Your son is breathing. I asked God about it. Your son is alive again.'

The mother said, 'That is really wonderful! Now I know you really are a man of God filled with God's power.

'Thank you, God,' she said, 'for sending Elijah to Zarephath so that I could learn how to trust you.'

The Lion Story Bible is made up of 52 individual
stories for young readers, building up an understanding
of the Bible as one story–God's story–a story for all
time and all people.

The Old Testament section (numbers 1-30) tells the story
of a great nation–God's chosen people, the Israelites–
and God's love and care for them through good times
and bad. The stories are about people who knew and
trusted God. From this nation came one special person,
Jesus Christ, sent by God to save all people everywhere.

Elijah asks for bread comes from the Old Testament,
first book of Kings, chapter 17. After King Solomon's
reign the kingdom split in two. The northern kingdom
of Israel, to which this story belongs, soon set up its
own places of worship and before long both king and
people were serving other gods. King Ahab's foreign
wife, Queen Jezebel, brought her own priests with her
and a temple to Baal was built in the capital city,
Samaria. The people who remained loyal to God were
persecuted. But God still loved his people. He sent
special messengers, the prophets, to try to turn them
back before it was too late. Elijah was one of the
greatest of all God's prophets.

The next book in the series, number 22: *Elijah and
the prophets of Baal,* tells the most dramatic story of
Elijah's eventful life.